Exstresso

Exstresso

TAKING A COFFEE BREAK WITH GOD

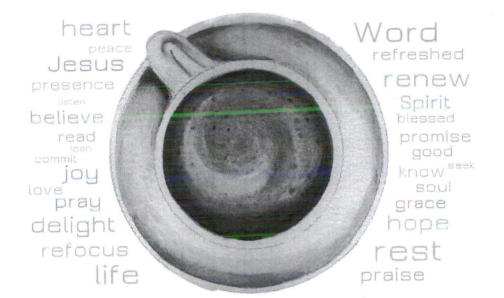

heart
peace
Jesus
presence
listen
believe
read
lean
commit
joy
love
pray
delight
refocus
life

Word
refreshed
renew
Spirit
blessed
promise
good
know seek
soul
grace
hope
rest
praise

LEAH WHITTON
with JESSICA CASAREZ

EXSTRESSO
published by 4:13 Press
© 2017 by Leah Whitton and Jessica Casarez

International Standard Book Number: 978-0-69296-669-3

Type set in Garamond, Black Jack, & Matilde Sketch.
Coffee cup stain graphic designed by Freepik.
Coffee cup and flower art by Laura Hayrapetyan.
Photos of the authors by Casey Jackson & John Mark Morgan II.

Italics in biblical quotes indicate emphasis added.
Unless otherwise indicated, all Scripture quotations are from the ESV® Bible (The
Holy Bible, English Standard Version®), copyright © 2001 by Crossway, a publishing
ministry of Good News Publishers. Used by permission. All rights reserved.

Published in the United States by 4:13 Press,
a division of Bammes Enterprises, LLC.

Printed in the United States of America

For information:
info@413press.com

Dedicated to PaPaw Francis

Jesus time and coffee time have been foundational building blocks in my life. You could say I was addicted to both as a child probably because my grandfather would take me to the coffee shop every day for donuts and coffee. I would drink out of his little saucer while he talked to me about life and most importantly, Jesus. Spending time with my grandfather in the mornings changed my life. I learned to listen, to share my heart, drink from a saucer, appreciate that nothing tastes better than warm donuts with coffee, and to love Jesus! I practiced taking a coffee break every day with God because of my Papaw.

I hope this devotional book will inspire you to take a break with Jesus every day, and as you do may God fill you with joy, peace, and calmness to overcome the stresses that life brings us.

I also want to thank my family for supporting my writing through their words of affirmation. I am amazingly blessed to have the best husband, children, and parents anyone could ask for.

– Leah

Contents

Preface

HOW TO USE THIS DEVOTIONAL

By Leah Whitton

I pray this book will challenge you to begin to take a short break with God every morning at your coffee table. The coffee table is a piece of furniture that is often overlooked in our homes—a place to set decorations or place our drinks—but through this study, perhaps it will find a place of greater importance in our homes and lives. My hope is that you will choose to sit at your coffee table at the beginning of each morning, trust God no matter what you are facing, and take a coffee break with God.

This book is organized into six weeks, each containing five days of devotionals. Each day has a short devotional, scripture references, a prayer for the day, and a few questions to help you reflect on what God is speaking to you. I like to call this the "STIR" method:

S =   Scripture

T =   Thoughts for the Day

I =   Invitation to Pray

R =   Respond

In our stress-filled world, I want to encourage you to STIR in a little time with Jesus every day. I pray you will enjoy this time as you meet with Jesus and release your life stresses to him.

The dream for this devotional started in prayer at a little coffee shop reminiscent of the coffee shops I visited with my grandfather as a child. As I began writing, I asked my good friend, Jessica Casarez, to contribute some of her devotionals to complement my own. Jessica and I love to talk about Jesus over a great cup of coffee (or for Jessica, two or three cups of coffee).

Week 1

LIVING STRESS-FREE
IN A STRESSED-OUT WORLD

Week 1: Day 1

STOP AND SMELL THE COFFEE

By Leah Whitton

Scripture Reading

[38] Now as they went on their way, Jesus entered a village. And a woman named Martha welcomed him into her house. [39] And she had a sister called Mary, who sat at the Lord's feet and listened to his teaching. [40] But Martha was distracted with much serving. And she went up to him and said, "Lord, do you not care that my sister has left me to serve alone? Tell her then to help me." [41] But the Lord answered her, "Martha, Martha, you are anxious and troubled about many things, [42] but one thing is necessary. Mary has chosen the good portion, which will not be taken away from her."

Luke 10:38-42

Thoughts for the Day

The living room was peaceful and quiet, except the sound of giggling inside a small pink tent in the back corner of the room. As I was spring cleaning, my daughter peeked her big blue eyes through an opening and quietly asked if I would play with her. "Not right now, Mommy is busy," I replied. A few minutes passed and my daughter eagerly asked again. In my mind, I knew that my to-do list was never-ending and stopping to play would only slow me down. Would I acquiesce and play with my daughter, or would I continue to work? I wrestled with this question, struggling to balance it all.

Do you ever face the same struggle?

Today's passage reminds us to slow down and remember what is most important. Mary chose to sit at Jesus's feet, while Martha was distracted with the many to-do items around the house.

I must admit, I am a Martha more than a Mary. I am guilty of starting my day consumed with the things I need to accomplish in the day ahead. I worry if I will accomplish everything for my kids, my husband, my work, and my church. I am like Martha, furiously going from task to task—always busy—but forgetting the most important thing: meeting with Jesus.

I heard this short story once from an anonymous author that makes me laugh every time I read it. This little grandmother was surprised by her seven-year-old grandson one morning. He had made her coffee. She drank what was the worst cup of coffee in her life. When she got to the bottom, there were three of those little green army men in the cup. She said, "Honey, what are the army men doing in my coffee?" Her grandson said, "Grandma, it says on TV, 'The best part of waking up is soldiers in your cup!'"

What if we woke up and started saying, "The best part of waking up... is Jesus with my cup?" Even Jesus himself took time to get away and spend some quiet time alone with his heavenly Father. We need to learn to prioritize our to-do list and place God at the very top. To do that, we must slow down, relax, and take time for what is important. I am not saying your to-do list is not important, nor am I saying it is bad. We certainly have items we must take care of each day, but when they consume us to the point that we miss meeting with God or enjoying time with a close family member, we may have missed the best for the good. Jesus said, "Martha chose good things to do, but Mary chose the better thing to do."

After remembering the story of Martha and Mary that morning while I was cleaning, I decided to put down my duster and ignore the clock. I grabbed some coffee and poured some in a little saucer for my daughter to drink from, just like my grandfather had done with me. Then we giggled together like a mother and daughter should. I slowed down that day, and it was absolutely worth it.

I must constantly remind myself to be like Mary. When we take time for those we love, it will not only fill their hearts, but ours as well. Just as my grandfather spent time with me on those early-morning donut and coffee trips, our Heavenly Father also desires to spend time each day with us. All we have to do is "draw near to God, and he will draw near to you" (James 4:8).

So, slow down today, open his Word, let him speak to you, and share your heart with him. Stop and smell the coffee.

Invitation to Prayer

Dear Lord: Help me slow down to spend time with you each day. I place my life in your hands and I desire to put you first before I start the rest of my to-do list for the day. Help me make this a priority and help me grasp how important it is to talk with and listen to you. May this change my life from this day forward. Amen.

Respond

- Has there been a time in your life when you have been so busy it feels like you are simply going through the motions?

- What keeps coming up that is preventing you from slowing down?

- How can you do a better job of choosing the best over the good?

Week 1: Day 2

COFFEE INVITE

By Leah Whitton

Scripture Reading

[1] He entered Jericho and was passing through. [2] And behold, there was a man named Zacchaeus. He was a chief tax collector and was rich. [3] And he was seeking to see who Jesus was, but on account of the crowd he could not, because he was small in stature. [4] So he ran on ahead and climbed up into a sycamore tree to see him, for he was about to pass that way. [5] And when Jesus came to the place, he looked up and said to him, "Zacchaeus, hurry and come down, for I must stay at your house today." [6] So he hurried and came down and received him joyfully. [7] And when they saw it, they all grumbled, "He has gone in to be the guest of a man who is a sinner." [8] And Zacchaeus stood and said to the Lord, "Behold, Lord, the half of my goods I give to the poor. And if I have defrauded anyone of anything, I restore it fourfold." [9] And Jesus said to him, "Today salvation has come to this house, since he also is a son of Abraham. [10] For the Son of Man came to seek and to save the lost."

Luke 19:1-10

Thoughts for the Day

Maybe you have heard the story of Zacchaeus in the Bible or remember the song: "Zacchaeus was a wee little man, and a wee little man was he." Can you finish the song? I remember singing this song as a child in Sunday school, and it has stuck in my head ever since. The story of Zacchaeus is all about love through a simple invite.

Zacchaeus was a tax collector, a despised profession often associated with corruption in that time and culture. One day, he heard Jesus was passing through his town, so he climbed up into a sycamore tree to see Jesus, because he was too short to see Jesus among the crowd. But the story took an unexpected turn: Jesus saw him and invited him to dinner.

The crowd around Jesus started to grumble. They didn't understand why Jesus would want to eat with such a corrupt person.

Zacchaeus accepted Jesus's invitation, and after meeting with Jesus, he gave half of his fortune to the poor and restored any mishandling of money fourfold. Wow! What a change in this man's life after accepting a simple invitation from Jesus. I love that when we meet with Jesus, it changes our life!

As pastors, we have received plenty of wedding invitations over the years. We love admiring all the beautiful decorations, eating scrumptious food, and enjoying the wonderful company. Recently, we received an invitation to our niece's wedding. On the invitation, there was a place to RSVP to respond whether you accept or decline the invitation. Did you know God sent us an invitation that was mailed a long time ago: an invitation to meet Jesus? Just like Zacchaeus, we don't deserve this invitation, but Jesus personally invites us anyway. We have the choice to accept or decline this invitation—to receive Jesus or reject him.

As Zacchaeus received Jesus into his home, we can receive Jesus into our hearts. What exactly does that mean? First, Zacchaeus acknowledged Jesus as Lord—the only one that really matters. Second, Zacchaeus repented (turned away from) of the wrong in his life and committed to live for Jesus from that day forward. But what Zacchaeus didn't know yet, is that Jesus would die on the cross to pay the penalty for our wrongs and then he would rise again to give us new life forever. When we receive Jesus, the power to "live for Jesus" comes not from ourselves, but from the cross.

Incredibly, if we would simply receive Jesus, he adopts us into his family and gives us access to everything he promised the "children of God" in his Word. John 14:18 says, "I will not leave you as orphans; I will come to you."

Maybe you have seen a family go through an adoption process. It is a beautiful thing to witness. It is much like how God adopts us. We take on his family name. He accepts us where we are and he loves us unconditionally. He protects us and converses with us through his Word and the Holy Spirit.

Have you accepted his invitation? Today, while sipping on your coffee or during your quiet time, think about if you have truly accepted the most important invitation you will ever get—one that will change your life forever.

If you have accepted the invitation, will you also share it with others so their lives can be changed forever as well?

Invitation to Prayer

Dear Lord: Thank you for inviting me to join your family. I accept your invitation and receive Jesus into my heart. You are the one that matters more than anyone else. I am sorry for the things I have done wrong. Help me each day as I willingly choose to live for you, and help me be bold enough to share with others your amazing invitation. I understand that once I accept your invitation, I am adopted into the family of God and receive all the benefits you have promised. Amen.

Respond

- Have you accepted God's invitation of salvation—to receive Jesus into your heart?

- If so, have you shared it with others? Who has God told you to share this good news with? Are you looking for opportunities to share?

- Luke 19:10 says, "For the Son of Man [that is, Jesus] came to seek and to save the lost." What does this scripture mean?

Week 1:
Day 3

COFFEE CONVERSATIONS

By Leah Whitton

Scripture Reading

[8] And the Lord called Samuel again the third time. And he arose and went to Eli and said, "Here I am, for you called me." Then Eli perceived that the Lord was calling the boy. [9] Therefore Eli said to Samuel, "Go, lie down, and if he calls you, you shall say, 'Speak, Lord, for your servant hears.'" So Samuel went and lay down in his place. [10] And the Lord came and stood, calling as at other times, "Samuel! Samuel!" And Samuel said, "Speak, for your servant hears." [11] Then the Lord said to Samuel, "Behold, I am about to do a thing in Israel at which the two ears of everyone who hears it will tingle.

1 Samuel 3:8-11

Thoughts for the Day

Most of us hit the ground running in the morning and go to bed completely exhausted at night, forgetting to have the most important conversation of the day. It takes intentional effort to set aside some time each day to have a conversation with God.

I remember after moving away from my grandfather in my teenage years, he was intentional about calling me at 8:00 am every Saturday morning to have a conversation with me. Although we couldn't meet for coffee at the donut store like we did when I was a child, he knew the importance of talking and listening to me on a consistent basis. He would give me advice and listen with an open heart. Most importantly, he would pray with me. I deeply miss my conversations with him, but I learned so much while he was here. I learned how to have conversations with people, and more importantly, with Jesus.

I often think about what it would be like if I had coffee with Jesus—with him physically sitting across from me. What would I ask? What would I do? I would hope I would listen just like Samuel did in the Bible.

John 10:27 states, "My sheep hear my voice, and I know them, and they follow me." In the book of 1 Samuel, Samuel heard God's voice audibly, listened to it, and obeyed it. God may not speak to me audibly like he did with Samuel, but I can hear his voice speaking to me through his Word and by the Holy Spirit. My prayers are not only me talking to God, but also listening with my heart and mind to hear his voice. I have a conversation with Him.

You will not get to know someone well unless you choose to spend time with him or her. It's not just about being in the same room with them though, you must actively engage in conversation. I can spend all day with my husband, but if I don't talk and listen to him, I will not grow closer to him.

My husband and I enjoy going to the movies and sharing a delicious bowl of buttery popcorn (if I choose to share), but I don't get to talk with him during the movie. We make it a point to talk after the movie about our favorite parts, things we learned, and scenes that didn't make sense. We choose to talk and listen to one another. It is about both quantity and quality time together.

Growing up, my parents knew the importance of this as well. I grew up in a military family that moved often across the states, but with all our relocations, my parents made it a priority to regularly take family camping trips. We would fish, play games, hike, and just spend time together. Those moments were all about quality and quantity time.

That is how it should be with God as well. In Isaiah 58:2, God describes what he desires from us: "They seek me daily and delight to know my ways,… they delight to draw near to God." You should converse with God often, and it should be about things on your heart and in his Word. Choose to grab some coffee and have a conversation with God today. Tell him the desires of your heart. Ask him to share new things from his Word and allow the Holy Spirit to speak to you. "Draw near to God, and he will draw near to you" (James 4:8a).

Invitation to Prayer

Dear Lord: I want to spend time with you in true engaging conversations. I want to know you so closely that I can hear and recognize your voice when you speak to my heart. Help me to intentionally and joyfully set aside time each day to wait and listen to you and to read your Word, so that I may know you more. Then also, give me the boldness and obedience to do what You say. Amen.

Respond

- Read 1 Samuel 3. What did Samuel need to do in order to hear God?

- Has there been a time where you sensed God was telling you to do something? Did you obey?

- What are you learning about God and about yourself in your prayer time?

Week 1: Day 4

A LATTE FUN

By Jessica Casarez

Scripture Reading

[26] For to the one who pleases him God has given wisdom and knowledge and joy, but to the sinner he has given the business of gathering and collecting, only to give to one who pleases God. This also is vanity and a striving after wind.

Ecclesiastes 2:26

Thoughts for the Day

I did not grow up in the church or with an understanding of what it truly meant to walk with God. When I finally did give my life to Christ, I thought I was giving up my "fun" life for a boring but safer life. But I was so wrong! You see, God does not want us to live a boring life. In fact, I honestly did not begin to live my life to the fullest until *after* I surrendered it to him. When I lived in darkness, I was caught up in a lot of sin. I did things according to my own desires, thinking any other kind of life would restrict me. I was so mistaken. My refusal to allow God to lead me caused me to suffer consequences for my bad decisions. It was my own way of living that ended up restricting me!

When I had enough of that lifestyle and I surrendered to him, the contrast in my life became obvious. If I thought I knew how to have fun before, my level of fun had just increased tremendously. The difference is that my pleasure and my fun now went hand-in-hand with freedom. I did not have to look over my shoulder all the time in fear. I could walk in freedom and with a heart full of joy while doing things that were not going to bring me harm or pain.

God wants us to have joy in our hearts. He wants us to enjoy life. In fact, he clearly tells us this in John 10:10: "I came that they may have life and have it abundantly." When Jesus came to us, he didn't just show up for a quick cup of coffee; he came primarily to die on the cross to pay the debt for our sin. That's how much God wants us to have eternal joy in him: he sacrificed his own life for it!

In the Psalms, David joyfully praises God, saying, "You make known to me the path of life; in your presence there is fullness of joy; at your right hand are pleasures forevermore" (Psalm 16:11). There is a huge difference between having fun in darkness and having fun in the light.

Are you having fun that pleases God? If this question scares you a bit, it may be time to examine how you are living your life. How are you measuring your happiness? I used to think the more people that liked me, the happier I would be. But I was doing things that completely went against the will of God and ultimately had destructive consequences. That is too high of a price to pay to find temporary happiness or have a few moments of empty fun.

All we have to do is live for him and in return he gives us an abundant life filled with wisdom and knowledge and joy.

Invitation to Prayer

Dear Lord: Help me find the joy and fun in getting to know you and living for you. I do not want to live a mundane life. Let others see a new joy in me that radiates brightly so they can see a life with you is not boring at all. Please stir me away from people or things that would distract me or discourage me from living for you. Amen.

Respond

- Are there any areas of your life where you need God to redefine "fun?" Is any of the "fun" you are having right now coming at a high cost? If so, ask God to show you if it is contrary to his will.

- What is the difference between having fun in the dark and having fun in the light?

- Have you ever found yourself intensely happy in God? Why or why not?

*Week 1:
Day 5*

LIQUID JOY

By Leah Whitton

Scripture Reading

[7] The Lord is my strength and my shield; in him my heart trusts, and I am helped; my heart exults, and with my song I give thanks to him.

Psalm 28:7

Thoughts for the Day

We seem to all be in the pursuit of happiness. We seek it through many different avenues: money, relationships, work, travel, popularity, and fame. However, pursuing happiness through the temporary things of this world will always ultimately leave us empty.

God didn't promise to make us happy in every moment of our life on earth, but he did promise that he would fill us with unquenchable joy. There is a big difference between being happy and being joyful. Happiness depends on your happenings (circumstances) in life. I'm happy when I get to shop at a jewelry store and actually buy something.

I am happy when my husband surprises me with dinner and a clean home. If things in life are going as planned, we are usually happy. If things are not going great, we are normally unhappy. I am unhappy when my child disobeys or is disrespectful. I am definitely unhappy when my coffeehouse is out of my favorite coffee.

One day I was complaining to an elderly widow in our church about my husband, Cecil, not picking up after himself. I was telling her that I get so tired of picking up his clothes that he leaves on the ground every night. I will never forget what she said: "My dear child, I would give anything just to have my husband's clothes laying on the ground again for me to pick up." Wow, talk about God using her words to humble me. You see, I was unhappy because my husband didn't pick up his clothes, but she knew joy of having her husband was far richer than my minor complaint. So, needless to say, I try not to complain about my husband anymore. I must admit, it has certainly helped our marriage be more joyful.

Paul tells us in Philippians that we can have joy regardless of the circumstances we are facing—whether we get a bad doctor's report, we lose a job, or a relationship we cherish begins to break.

Joy is not based on our circumstances. That is how joy and happiness are different. Paul states in Philippians 1:3-6: "I thank my God in all my remembrance of you, always in every prayer of mine for you all making my prayer with joy, because of your partnership in the gospel from the first day until now. And I am sure of this, that he who began a good work in you will bring it to completion at the day of Jesus Christ." Paul wrote these words from a prison cell. He was facing a trial before the emperor and a potential death sentence if found guilty, yet he was telling us that he is praying with *joy*. How?

You see, Paul understood that joy is not based on our circumstances, but in the security of knowing and trusting and exulting Jesus Christ.

We can rest knowing God will walk us through anything bad that could happen. The joy of having God is far richer than anything we will face in this life. We need to learn to focus on what really matters.

When I was young, my mom shared with me that if I put my hand right in front of my face and focus on my hand, everything else would become blurry. It is the same when we focus on God, all the peripheral happenings around us become blurry in comparison to him.

Are you focused on what really matters? Joy is based on a choice, and happiness is based on chance. You have a choice to walk in joy today. Nehemiah 8:10 declares that the "joy of the Lord is your strength." Choose joy today as you pray and reflect on all that God has done for you.

Invitation to Prayer

Dear Lord: I am so thankful that you offer us unceasing joy during the good times and the bad. I choose today to walk in the joy of knowing and trusting and praising you no matter what circumstances I face. I long for your supernatural joy that can only be found in you. Fill me to overflowing with your unquenchable joy. Amen.

Respond

- What is the main difference between happiness and joy? Can you think of a time you were especially happy and a time you were especially joyful?

- Can you think of a time you walked through a difficult time, but still had joy?

- What are the characteristics of someone who always has joy? How do they react to the happenings around them?

Week 2

THE DAILY GRIND

Week 2: Day 1

EXSTRESSO

By Leah Whitton

Scripture Reading

[5] Out of my distress I called on the Lord; the Lord answered me and set me free. [6] The Lord is on my side; I will not fear. What can man do to me?

Psalm 118:5-6

Thoughts for the Day

Have you ever been stressed? I would imagine most of us have been or currently are under a lot of stress. Life is stressful and messy at times.

When you combine "ex" with "stress," you get "ex-stress," which means without stress. How can we live without stress?

When we call out to God, he answers us and can help us live a life with less stress. One of the Greek words in the Bible for stress is *thlipsis*, which means pressure, burdens, affliction, or trouble. When Stephen was preaching in Acts 7:9-14 about Joseph from the Old Testament, he used the word *thlipsis* to describe Joseph's plight. If anyone had a right to be stressed, it was Joseph. He was sold into slavery by his brothers, wrongfully accused of rape by Pharaoh's wife, and thrown into prison and forgotten—all while being completely innocent and serving God. Joseph could have asked God: Where are you? Why have you left me?

Have you ever caught yourself asking those same questions? I know I have had times in my life where I had to go through extremely challenging, stressful, and heartbreaking situations, yet God was with me through each of those seasons.

In the year of 2001, I was pregnant with my first child. My husband and I were thrilled and anxious for our son's arrival. On December 27, around 10:00 p.m., something was about to change. We had not anticipated any problems—we expected joy, not stress--but suddenly our situation changed. Hudson was born with an aggressive infection called Strep B. This infection was so powerful it began to shut down every working system in his little body. The doctors estimated that he only had a 50% chance of survival. So, here we were, brand new parents, not knowing what to expect, and feeling the heartache of possibly losing our newborn son.

Hudson was placed in the NICU and was not improving. He was living on a respirator and IV antibiotics. The worst of it was that I was not able to hold him or touch him because it affected his blood pressure too much. I was at the end of my rope and I remember screaming out to God saying, "If you are really God, you will send someone here face-to-face to tell me audibly that my son will be healed and that he will come home with us."

That evening, a young pastor who we were friends with felt a strong sense that God was telling him to drive to our hospital. He wrestled a bit (especially because of the time and the distance) and he asked God if he could just call the hospital. "No," God said, "You must go." Around midnight that evening, this young pastor showed up in our hospital room. He told us God had woken him up and that he was supposed to come and tell me face-to-face that my child would live and he would come home with no complications. I called out to God in my stressful time and He answered my prayer in a powerful way. God showed himself faithful. The next day, Hudson began to improve and two weeks later came home 100% healthy.

During Joseph's distress, he called out to God. Joseph didn't allow stress to overwhelm him, and thus "God was with him and rescued him out of all his afflictions and gave him favor and wisdom before Pharaoh, king of Egypt, who made him ruler over Egypt and over all his household."

Joseph could have let stress swallow him up, but instead he brought his stress to God. Life will bring stress, but before letting that stress consume you, drink a good cup of God's "exstresso" (God's grace, mercy, and love) and allow him to bring healing to every area of your life. 1 Peter 5:7 tells us to "cast all your anxieties on him, because he cares for you." Hold on to that scripture when you walk through stressful times. God was with us through the horrible nightmare we faced when my son was born, and he will be with you also. Release your stress to him today and have a coffee conversation with God who is ready to carry your burdens.

Invitation to Prayer

Dear Lord: I admit I have carried the stresses of this life for too long and I need to hand them over to you. Stress has affected every area of my life and I feel consumed with worry and anxiety. When I am tempted to stress out about things I cannot control, help me to place them in your hands. I know you are always with me and will never let me go. Amen.

Respond

- How do you deal with stress?

- Read Psalm 118:5-6. What is God speaking to you through these verses?

- What are some things in your life right now that are stressing you out? What would it look like to surrender each of these stresses to God?

Week 2: Day 2

CAFÉ COURAGE

By Leah Whitton

Scripture Reading

[43] And there was a woman who had had a discharge of blood for twelve years, and though she had spent all her living on physicians, she could not be healed by anyone. [44] She came up behind him and touched the fringe of his garment, and immediately her discharge of blood ceased. [45] And Jesus said, "Who was it that touched me?" When all denied it, Peter said, "Master, the crowds surround you and are pressing in on you!" [46] But Jesus said, "Someone touched me, for I perceive that power has gone out from me." [47] And when the woman saw that she was not hidden, she came trembling, and falling down before him declared in the presence of all the people why she had touched him, and how she had been immediately healed. [48] And he said to her, "Daughter, your faith has made you well; go in peace."

Luke 8:43-48

Thoughts for the Day

Sometimes we live behind a mask hoping no one will see us. I know I feel that way when I go to the grocery store early in the morning with no makeup, a messy hair bun, and morning breath. I always see someone I know and try desperately to hide behind an aisle or my grocery basket. Ultimately, I generally end up having a complete conversation with my friend or a complete stranger. You would think I would have learned by now to get ready before I go out in public.

Just as we so often do today, this woman in the Bible hid behind a mask for many years, until one day she decided to courageously try to break free through the power of Jesus. We don't know her name, just that she had an issue related to persistent bleeding. For twelve long years, she was sick and none of the many physicians she visited could find a cure. In her culture, she was seen as unclean and an outcast. She lost everything and was literally put in isolation from everyone. Can you imagine? I know I complain if I am sick for just one day—I cannot imagine being sick for twelve long years!

We all have issues we must face and we all deal with them differently. This woman hid for a dozen years until one day she took a good dose of a cup of courage. She decided on one morning that she was going to do something different. She became desperate, and that desperation spilled into courage. She heard that Jesus was in her town and somehow she knew that where everyone else had failed, Jesus could finally heal her. She got up, hid amongst the crowd that gathered around Jesus, and did something brave: she reached out and touched the hem of Jesus's garment. You may be thinking, "What is so courageous about that?" Touching someone back in that time and culture when you were deemed unclean would be considered a death sentence. That's right: a death sentence! This woman was so desperate for a healing that courage and faith rose within her. She didn't care if she died from touching Jesus because she was desperate. She was going to do whatever it took to get her healing.

You see, so many people were touching Jesus at the same time this woman did, but something amazing happened when she touched Him. Jesus stopped and asked, "Who touched me?" People stood amazed because everyone around him was touching him, but Jesus knew someone had *touched* him—someone with a gigantic cup of faith and courage.

Because she courageously and desperately reached for Jesus in faith, this woman was immediately healed—one touch is all it took. One touch is all it takes for us as well.

You might have problems that you have been dealing with for years. At the very least, all of us started life desperately sick in our hearts. To heal us, Jesus went a step further than simply acting as a physician. *He* bled for us on the cross, and "with his wounds we are healed" (Isaiah 53:5). All it takes is a little courage and faith to reach out for Jesus. One touch can set you free.

Will you reach out to Jesus today? Will you gather your courage and faith to turn to him instead of continually hiding behind a mask?

Invitation to Prayer

Dear Lord: Today I choose to have the courage to trust you regardless of the situation or outcome. I admit I have been battling with certain issues for a long time and I need a healing touch from you. I need a touch (spiritually, mentally, physically, emotionally) from you today and I am reaching out now in faith that you will heal me, mend me, and make me more like you today. Amen.

Respond

- Has there been a time in your life where your faith was increased?

- Is there an area in your life (spiritually, physically, mentally, emotionally) that you have been battling with? Will you reach out to Jesus for healing instead of facing it alone?

- Do you have a place in your life you haven't allowed God to touch and heal? Are there any areas of your life where you are still hiding behind a mask?

Week 2: Day 3

CAREFREE SYRUP

By Leah Whitton

Scripture Reading

[7] casting all your anxieties on him, because he cares for you.

1 Peter 5:7

Thoughts for the Day

Receiving bad news is never easy and it can leave us feeling anxious, overwhelmed, and fearful. About a year ago, I received some alarming and unexpected news. I had gone for my yearly health check-up at the doctor's office. No big deal. But then I was told that they found a mass in my left breast. Immediately fear rose inside of me and I started to panic. My mom and aunt had both had breast cancer, and anxiety started consuming me. I had to catch my breath, calm the flood of worry, and just pray. If I had faced this a few years earlier, I would not have handled it so well. When fear and anxiety attacked me in the past, I used to cave into a vicious cycle of panic attacks that affected me emotionally, spiritually, and physically.

I have learned a lot over the past few years on how to handle fearful situations. I have to remind myself of one of my favorite stories in the Bible. Perhaps you have heard the story about an Old Testament king who dealt with anxiety, learned to overcome it, and ultimately defeated great armies because he knew where to place his trust. His name was Jehoshaphat and his story is found in 2 Chronicles 20.

The nations were coming against Israel and Jehoshaphat was afraid, but he did something that we all need to learn: He humbled himself and immediately surrendered the situation to the Lord. In verse 12, he simply states that he didn't know what to do, but he fixed his eyes on the Lord.

I didn't know what to do when faced with a scary doctor's report, but I quickly focused my attention on God. As I began to pray and change my focus, God brought a sense of calm to my heart even in the middle of my situation. In the end, it turned out after several MRI's and a biopsy, that my mass was benign (praise God)!

1 Peter 5:7 says, "Cast all your anxieties on him, because he cares for you." In this verse, "cast" is translated from the Greek word *epiripto*, which means to forcefully throw something.

Our bodies were not designed to carry all of these heavy anxieties. We must learn to throw them off of us. Pay attention to the second word in this verse: "all." God doesn't ask us to cast some, a little, a few, or none—he said, "Cast *all* your anxieties on him." We should give all our thoughts, anxieties, and worries to God. God is infinitely more capable of carrying our burdens than us, and God loves us and deeply cares about everything you are going through. He cares about every detail in our lives, big or small.

Our reaction to fearful or stressful moments is very important. Are we going to shrink back in fear or are we willing to hand it *all* over to God? One choice will allow you to live in freedom and the other will imprison you. Which one will you decide? Grab some coffee this morning and add a little carefree syrup in your prayer time. Read 2

Chronicles 20 and reflect on Jehoshaphat's story to encourage you as you walk in freedom from your anxieties.

Invitation to Prayer

Dear Lord: I thank you that I don't have to carry my burdens and anxieties alone. You are always ready to take them from me. I have carried them for too long and it is affecting my emotions, my health, my relationships, and even my everyday tasks. I choose today to cast my cares on you and walk in freedom from the anxiety and worries that have tormented me. I choose to have joy knowing these situations are in your strong and loving hands. Amen.

Respond

- How can you let go of your daily worries?

- Instead of worrying, what can you focus on?

- What does it mean to keep looking at God (2 Chronicles 20:12)?

Week 2: Day 4

COFFEE BAGS

By Leah Whitton

Scripture Reading

22 For I am poor and needy, and my heart is stricken within me. 26 Help me, O Lord my God! Save me according to your steadfast love!

Psalm 109:22,26

Thoughts for the Day

"One of my favorite chores is taking out the garbage," said no one ever. The truth is we don't like to carry messy garbage from the kitchen to the garage, let alone lug it around with us as we go from place to place! But if we are honest, some of us carry messy baggage around with us all day, everyday. We may not see it with our physical eyes, but the baggage is there. The baggage of hurt words, sin, betrayal, addictions, depression, anxiety, abuse—and the list could go on.

In Psalm 109:22, King David shows us that he relates to those of us carrying unnecessary baggage around. "For I am poor and needy, and my heart is stricken within me." How many of us feel like that at times?

Heartbroken. Crushed. Discouraged. Acknowledge your pain and your baggage and give it to the only one who can fix it.

In this Psalm, David reminds us what we need to do when we carry baggage around. Verse 26 says, "Help me, O Lord my God! Save me according to your steadfast love!" We need to acknowledge that we need help from a Savior who will lift our messy baggage off us just like King David.

For many of us, we want to keep our baggage hidden and not deal with it. We often carry it around and let it weight us down. So first, we must come to a place where we recognize our own baggage so that we can hand it completely over to God. Carrying baggage will only leave you tired, hurt, weary, and confused.

King David knew he could trust God to help him. Look at verse 31 of the same chapter, "For he [the Lord] stands at the right hand of the needy one, to save him from those who condemn his soul to death."

We need to trust God completely just like David. God is waiting for you to ask him to carry your burdens.

In Matthew 11, Jesus tell us, "Come to me, all who labor and are heavy laden, and I will give you rest. Take my yoke upon you, and learn from me, for I am gentle and lowly in heart, and you will find rest for your souls. For my yoke is easy, and my burden is light" (v. 28-30). God reminds us that he is the burden/baggage lifter. Will you bring your baggage to Him today? God specializes in restoring your life by taking the baggage off and replacing it with his "easy yoke" of love, joy, faith, and obedience. God is inviting you to surrender your mistakes, your sins, your past failures, your anxieties, your hurt, and your pain. Grab your coffee and take off the messy baggage you have been carrying. He will replace it with his grace, strength, and love.

Invitation to Prayer

Dear Lord: I come before you today thanking you for being the God who listens to my prayers. I admit that I have been carrying around unnecessary baggage for too long. I surrender everything to you today, even the baggage that I have kept hidden from others. I want you to fill my heart with your love and joy so that I can walk in a new freedom, without the heavy burdens I've been carrying. I am tired of being weary and hurt and weighed down. I need a touch from you to restore my heart. Amen.

Respond

- What unnecessary baggage are you carrying?

- Have you fully given everything (your past, your thoughts, your emotions, your actions) over to God?

- Reflect on Matthew 11:30. What is God is speaking to you?

Week 2: Day 5

MORNING BREATH

By Leah Whitton

Scripture Reading

²¹ Death and life are in the power of the tongue, and those who love it will eat its fruits.

Proverbs 18:21

Thoughts for the Day

One morning my youngest boy, Houston, came and gave me a big hug after a night when he had been feeling sick. When he reached over and got close to my face, his breath smelled incredibly awful. It was so bad that my eyes started to water and my stomach was cringing. I gave him a quick hug and led him directly to the bathroom sink so he could brush his teeth.

Many times, when we are physically sick, our breath stinks badly. Sometimes when we are spiritually sick, our breath can stink as well. The words that come out of our mouth can truly change the atmosphere to either a pleasant one or an awful one. Words are very powerful: You can either breathe life into someone or you can breathe death.

Proverbs 18:21 says, "Death and life are in the power of the tongue." We have the power to build people up or tear people down. It truly is a choice based on the words we choose to speak. The Bible says that the tongue is like a bit in a horse's mouth or a rudder on a ship—it is so tiny, but it commands the direction of something so enormous (James 3:3-4). Therefore, our words have the power to shape the course of our lives. We can choose to allow our words to steer us in the right direction by speaking uplifting, life-changing words.

Think about how God created the world: He *spoke* the universe into existence. His words literally produced life. While our own words obviously don't carry the same weight as God's, the point is clear: Spoken words have a tremendous power. Words can bring comfort or they can bring devastation.

This is something we all need to keep working on.

First, we can change the quality of our speech by focusing on the contents of our hearts. Maybe you have heard Luke 6:45: "For out of the abundance of the heart his mouth speaks." Our hearts need to be changed by God first. We need the power of the cross to "remove the heart of stone… and give us a heart of flesh" (Ezekiel 36:26). Then we need to ask the Holy Spirit to help clean our hearts and fill it with the things of God. Philippians 4:8 says, "Finally, brothers, whatever is true, whatever is honorable, whatever is just, whatever is pure, whatever is lovely, whatever is commendable, if there is any excellence, if there is anything worthy of praise, think about these things." When we do this, the words that come out of our mouths will bring life because the contents of our hearts are pure.

Second, we need to learn to control our tongues. Whether it is at our job, in our family, or in church—gossip, slander, being a busy-body, or judgmental tears people down and causes division and friction. Sometimes we get so super-spiritual when it comes to gossip. Maybe you have used this line, "I'm just telling you this so that you can pray about it." There are no excuses; gossip grieves the Spirit of God.

My husband has used this phrase many times as a pastor, "If you are not a part of the problem or the solution, you don't need to be talking about it to someone else."

Lastly, our morning breath should be quieted in order to hear the Holy Spirit talking to us. Sometimes we talk too much about us that we don't hear what God is trying to teach or tell us. To hear the Holy Spirit, we need to close our mouths and listen. So, today choose to fill your heart with God's love and let the words out of your mouth be uplifting to all those around you. Check your heart, your motivation, and your words. Ask God to help you change them today to line up with God's heart and his Word.

Invitation to Prayer

Dear Lord: I thank you for speaking to my heart today. I need a touch from you to change the content of my heart. Forgive me for the times when I have hurt others through my words. Give me the power to control my words, so that they may be uplifting instead of damaging. Help me to close my ears when others around me gossip and close my mouth when I am tempted to gossip. Above all, I will use my mouth to praise you for who you are and for your love shown to me on the cross. Amen.

Respond

- Have you ever experienced a time where you spoke negative words and later regretted it? Was the damage was already done? Did you do anything to correct it?

- What do you think makes people want to gossip about others? Why is it harmful?

- Reflect on Proverbs 18:21. How do your words have the power of life or death?

Week 3

GROUNDED IN HIS WORD

Week 3: Day 1

BREWTIFUL WORD

By Jessica Casarez

Scripture Reading

[105] Your word is a lamp to my feet and a light to my path. [106] I have sworn an oath and confirmed it, to keep your righteous rules. [107] I am severely afflicted; give me life, O Lord, according to your word! [108] Accept my freewill offerings of praise, O Lord, and teach me your rules. [109] I hold my life in my hand continually, but I do not forget your law. [110] The wicked have laid a snare for me, but I do not stray from your precepts.

Psalm 119:105-110

Thoughts for the Day

We live in a world where we have so many things easily accessible at our fingertips.

We need to try and figure out how to whip up dinner in 20 minutes with the only three ingredients we have in the pantry? No problem! We can type the ingredients in a search box and will be instantly shown at least ten different recipes.

Our familiar route to work is interrupted with construction threatening to make us late? No problem! Our faithful GPS will immediately find the best alternative routes for us.

This method of having fast solutions may start to "spoil" us if we think the same strategies can be applied to every situation. What happens when your marriage is attacked and you and your spouse can barely stand to be in the same room? What do you do when suddenly your children seem to be drawing further away from you and from God? Is there an app on your phone that can immediately get everything back on track?

Things around us are constantly changing. There never seems to be *one* permanent solution. As soon as you buy the perfect phone case for your smartphone, a new generation gets released. Somehow the remedies you used last fall for your allergies no longer work.

But there is one constant that can be applied to every situation—one that is always true and never expires. It is the Scriptures—the Word of God. Psalm 119 tells us that the Word of God can light up our dark path. We don't have to stumble around and try to get back right on track. His Word is our perfect map and our unfailing compass!

I remember when I was a new Christian I had so many doubts about whether God really heard me. I envisioned him with something like an email account with millions of unread e-mails. I mean, I was sure everyone was sending him messages. Did he really have time to hear from me? Did he even *want* to hear from me? The answers are YES and YES!

The problem was not whether God could hear me. It was whether I was actually paying attention to *listen* to Him. A lamp is useless if it is not lit. It can look like a lamp on the outside but it won't do what it needs to do until it is turned on.

The same thing can be said of God Word in our lives. Our Bible can remain on our shelf gathering dust and looking pretty. But it cannot and will not do what it needs to do until you open it and begin to ask God to help you understand it and use it, so it will be your light in every situation.

Invitation to Prayer

Dear Lord: Help me to treasure your Word and read it at least a little each day. Every time I read and study the Bible, give me understanding so the words I read would help me know and enjoy and trust you more. Then, remind me of your Word throughout each day, and use what I've read to be my light through every situation, no matter how dark. I thank you hearing me and for speaking to me. Amen.

Respond

- When you are faced with heavy and overwhelming problems in your life, is God the first person you go to? Why or why not?

- What can you do to help ensure you are actively listening to God's voice and instructions in your life?

- Are you frequently reminded of Bible verses that help you throughout your day? If not, what can you do to let God's Word light up your path more brightly?

Week 3: Day 2

THIRSTY

By Leah Whitton

Scripture Reading

[13] Jesus said to her, "Everyone who drinks of this water will be thirsty again, [14] but whoever drinks of the water that I will give him will never be thirsty again. The water that I will give him will become in him a spring of water welling up to eternal life." [15] The woman said to him, "Sir, give me this water, so that I will not be thirsty or have to come here to draw water."

John 4:13-15

Thoughts for the Day

Have you ever been thirsty? I mean really thirsty. Before my husband and I were married, he took a trip to Sudan for a missions trip. While passing out Bibles on this trip, he was arrested and put in a small jail cell in the middle of the desert for three days. He became extremely thirsty in the blistering heat. When they finally brought him some water, it had been taken straight from the Nile River. It was brown and filled with unimaginable debris, but he didn't care. He was so thirsty, he drank it all.

In our Scripture today, God says that if we will take a drink of his water, we will never thirst again, but what does that mean?

Let's first look at whom he was talking to in these verses. Many of us know her as the woman at the well. The life she was living was leaving her dry. She was an insecure adulterer, looking for meaning in one relationship after another. But then Jesus showed up. The first thing God shows us from this story is that Jesus goes to great lengths to meet us where we are.

Where are you right now with your relationship with God? If you feel far away from God just like the woman at the well, I have good news: Jesus will go to great lengths to meet you here and now. Why? Simple: He loves you!

Do you remember John 3:16? He came to us and he continues to come to us. Let's look back at John 4:4: "And he [Jesus] had to pass through Samaria." The Bible says that Jesus was traveling from Judea to Galilee, but between Judea and Galilee there was a place called Samaria. Jesus chose to go through Samaria. Seems logical, right? But what is extraordinary about this is that normally Jewish travelers would go out of their way to *avoid* going through Samaria. You see, Jews at the time shunned Samaritans since they had taken on other religious practices that were not from God. So, Jews always avoided Samaria. But not Jesus. He is an out-of-the-ordinary kind of God. He goes to great lengths to meet people where they are, and he still does.

Jesus shows us in this passage that he truly knows our deepest needs. He knows our hurts, our desires, and our hopes. John 4 goes on to say, "It was about the sixth hour [noon]. A woman from Samaria came to draw water" (v. 6b-7a). This was a different hour than usual. Normally women would go to the well together in the early morning so they could socialize (wells were the original water coolers) and because it would get too hot to go later in the day. Perhaps this Samaritan woman went at noon time because of her insecurity, her fear, or her shame.

Maybe she felt others would judge her. Maybe she felt like an outcast. I am sure some of us can relate. Perhaps you go to work and hide in your cubicle just to avoid talking to someone? Or maybe you avoid crowds because of a poor self-image or insecurity?

Growing up I had a horrible speech impediment. It was so bad that my own mother could not understand me. Many times, I just wanted to crawl under my bed so I didn't have to talk to anyone. Jesus knew my insecurities, just like he knows yours.

Jesus knew the insecurities of the woman at the well. He knew her past and her present, and yet he still wanted to meet with her and show her his unconditional love and the security that could only be found in him. Jesus wanted to satisfy her deepest needs. In verses 13-15, Jesus offered her living water. She came to the well looking for temporary satisfaction (she'd have to return to the well again tomorrow), but after talking to Jesus, she left feeling eternally satisfied. That's what it means to never thirst again. When we receive Jesus, our thirst for other things disappears as he forever satisfies our deepest longings.

He wants to do the same with you.

I heard an illustration once that beautifully portrays this. Imagine you are in a dry and hot desert with no water left in your canteen. Suddenly you come across an old water pump with a jug of water sitting beside it. On the jug was written this note, "Pour all the water into the pump to get all the water you need." What would you do? You are so thirsty that you are tempted by the immediate satisfaction of drinking the water in the jug. But do you instead trust the note and pour the entire jug into the pump? If you decide to pour the water into the pump, it would prime the pump so that water would continually come out of the pump in a seemingly endless supply. But if you just drink the water in the jug, you'd soon be thirsty again with nowhere to turn. If you knew the pump would supply endless water, this would certainly be an easy decision!

It is just like that in our spiritual lives. Are you willing to give up temporary pleasures that will always leave you thirsty for more, in order to gain joy and peace and life that will never end? If you have confidence in the eternal promises of God, the choice is easy. As missionary Jim Elliot once wrote, "He is no fool who gives what he cannot keep, to gain what he cannot lose."

But how can you be sure that God's promises are true? "He who did not spare his own Son but gave him up for us all, how will he not also with him graciously give us all things?" (Romans 8:32).

Invitation to Prayer

Dear Lord: I admit that I have been dry. I have been filling my life up with immediate satisfactions that are always leaving me empty. I want you to fill me to overflowing, so I don't want anything else but you. I have been weary and tired, and I need a touch from you today to give me a fresh start. Will you come close to me and hold me today as I reach out to you? Thank you, God, for loving me despite my faults and failures. I give my heart to you. Move me out of the way and make room in my heart for the eternal spring of living water that only you can supply. Amen.

Respond

- What are you truly thirsty for? Are there thirsts in your life that are crowding out your thirst for God?

- Read Psalm 42:1. What does it mean for your soul to "thirst for God?"

- What does Jesus mean that you will never thirst again in John 4:13-15?

Week 3: Day 3

ON THE ROCKS

By Jessica Casarez

Scripture Reading

[1] That same day Jesus went out of the house and sat beside the sea. [2] And great crowds gathered about him, so that he got into a boat and sat down. And the whole crowd stood on the beach. [3] And he told them many things in parables, saying: "A sower went out to sow. [4] And as he sowed, some seeds fell along the path, and the birds came and devoured them. [5] Other seeds fell on rocky ground, where they did not have much soil, and immediately they sprang up, since they had no depth of soil, [6] but when the sun rose they were scorched. And since they had no root, they withered away. [7] Other seeds fell among thorns, and the thorns grew up and choked them. [8] Other seeds fell on good soil and produced grain, some a hundredfold, some sixty, some thirty. [9] He who has ears, let him hear."...

[18] "Hear then the parable of the sower: [19] When anyone hears the word of the kingdom and does not understand it, the evil one comes and snatches away what has been sown in his heart. This is what was sown along the path. [20] As for what was sown on rocky ground, this is

the one who hears the word and immediately receives it with joy, [21] yet he has no root in himself, but endures for a while, and when tribulation or persecution arises on account of the word, immediately he falls away. [22] As for what was sown among thorns, this is the one who hears the word, but the cares of the world and the deceitfulness of riches choke the word, and it proves unfruitful. [23] As for what was sown on good soil, this is the one who hears the word and understands it. He indeed bears fruit and yields, in one case a hundredfold, in another sixty, and in another thirty."

Matthew 13:1-9,18-23

Thoughts for the Day

Have you ever noticed how much easier it is to praise God and trust God when we have money in our bank accounts, our entire family is healthy, and everything seems to be going in our favor? The problem with living a life like that is that it is not at all what God requires or asks.

He wants us to live a life that emulates him at *all* times—in sickness or in health, for richer or for poorer. This means that we continue trusting God even when all odds seem to be stacked against us. This means that we rejoice in him even when we don't receive the news we were expecting. This means we continue loving people even when they have hurt us. This is what he commands, and this is what he deserves.

Look closely at what the Scripture here is describing. Anyone can casually read or listen to the Word of God just as anyone can try and plant a crop. But there are other critical factors that determine whether anything will grow. We must make sure that we are rooted in faith that God's Word and his promises are absolutely true. Just like plants require good soil, we as people require good ground for the Word to grow within us.

How do we do this? How do we make sure that the Word of God is growing within us?

We must be diligent and consistent in reading the Bible and spending time in prayer, so that we know and understand his Word and his promises. This is the planting, and without the planting there can be no growing.

But we must also continually remind ourselves that God's Word is unconditionally true and his promises are better than anything else we could hope or imagine. "And now, O Lord God, you are God, and your words are true, and you have promised this good thing to your servant." (2 Samuel 7:28). This is the fertilizing—enriching the soil so what is planted can grow.

When I do not take the time to apply these simple instructions, I become the perfect example of the path where the seeds were stolen or the rocky or thorny ground where the seeds could not properly grow.

I can kick-start my day with a cup of coffee and have a long and detailed to-do list, but if I do not take the time to read and pray, I become easy prey. My kids will drive me crazier than usual. I will magnify my husband's imperfections. I will view interruptions as inconveniences rather than necessary breaks.

His Word is not optional, it is necessary.

Invitation to Prayer

Dear Lord: I ask you to please help me hunger for you every single day. Let my walk with you not be an option, but instead an everlasting and overwhelming desire in my heart! As I cannot survive without putting food and water in my body, remind me that I cannot live without putting your Word inside of me. May I meditate and reflect on it so I can clearly hear you. May I trust you above anyone or anything else, that nothing would rob me of the joy and security that can only be found in you. Even when troubles come, I want to stand tall and rejoice knowing and trusting that you go before me. Amen.

Respond

- Is there anything in your life that triggers you to jump into a state of anger or depression or worry or fear? How can you fully surrender that to God so it can no longer be used against you?

- What is something you can do to ensure you not only become rooted in the Word of God but also remain rooted throughout every day and every year?

Week 3:
Day 4

STIR IN THE ARMOR OF GOD

By Leah Whitton

Scripture Reading

[10] Finally, be strong in the Lord and in the strength of his might. [11] Put on the whole armor of God, that you may be able to stand against the schemes of the devil. [12] For we do not wrestle against flesh and blood, but against the rulers, against the authorities, against the cosmic powers over this present darkness, against the spiritual forces of evil in the heavenly places. [13] Therefore take up the whole armor of God, that you may be able to withstand in the evil day, and having done all, to stand firm. [14] Stand therefore, having fastened on the belt of truth, and having put on the breastplate of righteousness, [15] and, as shoes for your feet, having put on the readiness given by the gospel of peace. [16] In all circumstances take up the shield of faith, with which you can extinguish all the flaming darts of the evil one; [17] and take the helmet of salvation, and the sword of the Spirit, which is the word of God,

Ephesians 6:10-17

Thoughts for the Day

Growing up as a child, I loved to watch cartoons about superheroes. I loved to see the good guys or girls win. I even had a Wonder Woman outfit I would wear as I pretended to save the world. There was just something about putting on Wonder Woman's cape that made me feel like I could conquer anything.

That was all childhood fun, but God wants to equip us with spiritual armor (an outfit), so we can fight and conquer the enemy of our souls that wants to destroy us.

Too often we are fighting the wrong opponent. We often think our opponent is our boss at work, our spouse during an argument, or perhaps that family member you haven't spoken to in ages. But the devil is the one we need to be fighting and he wages warfare against our family and us all the time.

One of the keys to a successful battle is to know your enemy. 1 Peter 5:8 says, "Your adversary the devil prowls around like a roaring lion, seeking someone to devour." The devil will do everything he can to stalk you, intimidate you, and torment you. He looks for weaknesses and tries to exploit them. If we do not equip ourselves correctly, the devil can easily speak lies to us that we start to believe, leading to a vicious cycle spiraling down the wrong path.

2 Corinthians 10:3-4 states, "For though we walk in the flesh, we are not waging war according to the flesh. For the weapons of our warfare are not of the flesh, but have divine power to destroy strongholds." In these powerful verses, Paul speaks to us about spiritual warfare. He tells us that God has given weapons to use in battle for offensive and defensive purposes to defeat the enemy. The devil has a plan to attack you and you must know how to spiritually fight back.

God tells us in Ephesians 6:11 to put on the full armor of God— not just a few pieces, but *everything* that God gives us to equip us for battle. Put on the belt of truth (which is knowing the truth and standing upon it no matter what), the breastplate of righteousness (seeking God's righteousness, not our own), shoes (sharing the gospel with others and also standing firm when the devil attacks), the shield of faith (to protect you from the darts of the enemy), the helmet of salvation (to protect against the mental assaults of the enemy), and the sword of the spirit (which is the Word of God, the only offensive weapon mentioned).

Today, maybe you are facing a difficult situation in your home, at your work, or with a loved one. Remember who your real enemy is: the devil. Suit up for battle daily, and walk in victory because you know who has your back. "Take up the whole armor of God, that you may be able to withstand in the evil day, and having done all, to stand firm" (Ephesians 6:13). Remember, "in all these things we are more than conquerors through him who loved us" (Romans 8:37).

Invitation to Prayer

Dear Lord: Thank you for providing me with everything I need to withstand the devil and his attacks. Help me to concentrate my fight on the true opponent, the devil, who you have already defeated by your death and resurrection. I know I cannot face this enemy on my own. I need your power and the weapons you have given me to overcome every plan the devil has for me and my family. I suit up today with the whole armor of God and choose to walk in confidence in every battle I face. Amen.

Respond

- Who are you fighting against according to 2 Corinthians 10:3-4? What does this tell you about the specific everyday battles you face?

- Read Romans 8:28-39. How are you "more than a conqueror?"

Week 3: Day 5

BROKEN COFFEE CUP

By Leah Whitton

Scripture Reading

[36] One of the Pharisees asked him to eat with him, and he went into the Pharisee's house and reclined at table. [37] And behold, a woman of the city, who was a sinner, when she learned that he was reclining at table in the Pharisee's house, brought an alabaster flask of ointment, [38] and standing behind him at his feet, weeping, she began to wet his feet with her tears and wiped them with the hair of her head and kissed his feet and anointed them with the ointment. [39] Now when the Pharisee who had invited him saw this, he said to himself, "If this man were a prophet, he would have known who and what sort of woman this is who is touching him, for she is a sinner."

Luke 7:36-39

Thoughts for the Day

Have you ever broken something really valuable? I won't ever forget the devastating day I broke my sister's coffee cup that we had bought together a few months before she passed away. I lost my sister in a tragic drunk driving accident in 2012 and that coffee cup had been a reminder of the good times we shared over cups of coffee. When I dropped that cup, it brought back the terrible memory of the accident, as if I replayed the entire thing in my head. I looked down at the cup and I realized that I was just like that cup that was lying on the ground, shattered in pieces desperately wanting to be put back together again.

After the wreck, I was broken and hurt. I questioned God. I wanted answers. I wanted to feel again. I became numb to everyone around me. Perhaps you have felt the same way at some point in your life. I had to acknowledge that I was broken and needed to be put back together again. But how? I was shattered. I was a mess. All I could think about was how I would never be the same after losing my one and only sibling.

God chooses to heal each of us in his own way. He chose to heal me over time with little gestures of his great love for me. A few days after the funeral, I received a phone call from my mom. We had given some items to a donation center after my sister's passing. The donation center had called my mom to tell her that they had found an important letter addressed to the family. Somehow, we had missed it as we sorted through my sister's belongings. The envelope read, "In case I die, please read." I was shocked to find that she had written such a message. When I opened that letter, she had a message for me and I could hear her fun-loving voice talking through this letter. It was her way of saying goodbye to all of us. Needless to say, this letter brought comfort to all and I believe God orchestrated it to bring healing to my broken heart.

Are you broken and hurt? Maybe you have been shattered by a broken marriage or relationship, a broken dream, a broken life, or a broken heart. Perhaps you are like the woman found in Luke 7:36-39, who was broken and desperate for a touch from Jesus. She came to Jesus and poured oil from her alabaster box on his head, washed His feet with her tears, and wiped them with her hair. The cost of the oil was lavish, but she knew who was in the room and how much he was worth. She knew she was a sinner and fell at Jesus's feet needing forgiveness.

She was broken. She was tired. Even the others in the room spoke in hushed tones about her and spoke up incredulously that such a sinner would be allowed in the same room as Jesus.

I love Jesus's response. He loved her and responded immediately with compassion. He gave her his attention, forgave her, restored her, and even commended her for her love.

Jesus still does that with us today. No matter how broken you are or how much sin rules your life, Jesus loves you and wants to bring healing, forgiveness, and restoration to you.

When we fall short, when we feel ashamed and broken. But, we can always fall at the feet of Jesus asking him to put us back together again. And incredibly, he always does. I want to remind you today that you are never too broken for repair. You are never too shattered that God can't put you back together again. I picked up that broken coffee cup that day, put the pieces on my coffee table, and started slowly putting the cup back together.

Jesus will do the same for you. When we are broken, he can restore, repair, and renew. Let him.

Invitation to Prayer

Dear Lord: I come to you today because I am broken. I have been hurt and I don't know how to put the pieces of my life back together again. I don't have much to give to you except some broken pieces, but I trust you with them. Heal my heart today and let me feel your loving arms around me. Thank you for loving me even when I am broken, for carrying me when I don't think I can make it, and for turning my brokenness into something beautiful—a testimony of your unfailing goodness. Amen.

Respond

- Do you feel broken and hurt? What do you need to turn over to Jesus today?

- Has God ever turned something broken in your life into something beautiful?

Week 4

PRESSING THROUGH

Week 4: Day 1

PRESSED, BUT NOT CRUSHED

By Jessica Casarez

Scripture Reading

[8] We are afflicted in every way, but not crushed; perplexed, but not driven to despair;

2 Corinthians 4:8

Thoughts for the Day

Some days I feel as if everything in my world is falling apart. My husband and I seem to be speaking different languages to one another. My kids want to challenge me on every single thing I ask them to do, from cleaning their rooms to stopping their bickering. Our finances seem scarce and the report from the doctor is not as good as I had hoped. In times like this, it would be so easy to fall apart. But how would that be a demonstration of my faith?

My faith in God is not based on what is happening *to* me; it is based on what has happened *for* me. Before anything else, my faith starts with the cross: "What then shall we say to these things? If God is for us, who can be against us? He who did not spare his own Son but gave him up for us all, how will he not also with him graciously give us all things" (Romans 8:31-32)? Therefore, "we know that for those who love God all things work together for good, for those who are called according to his purpose" (Romans 8:28).

I have learned to acknowledge that God does not waste anything that happens. We can take something good from it and learn and grow from it. When my marriage is struggling, I must really push my pride to the side and ask myself: Is there something I need to ask forgiveness for? Or do I need to forgive my spouse for something I am still holding against him? How can we improve our communication? Ladies, believe it or not, men cannot always read our minds and sometimes we can help our marriages a lot by simply telling them plainly what we need to tell them.

When my kids are acting crazy, I seek God's wisdom in how to raise and correct my children. When my finances look scarce, I choose to fully trust that God will provide for everything that we need—and He always does. My worrying does nothing to help the situation but rather discourages me and distracts me from doing things that matter.

I want to be a parent and a person who truly teaches that we can FULLY trust the Lord in every situation. But how can I preach that when I am having a difficult time living by those words? Has God not proven his faithfulness over and over? I know He is able and I know his ways are so much higher than my ways.

Invitation to Prayer

Dear Lord: I thank you for always being my comfort. I know you did not promise us that life would be completely free of pain or trouble. I want to be more aware of making you my only source instead of just a back-up plan. Who can compare to you, my Father? When everything around me seems to be crumbling, help me remember that nothing can strip me from your love and your Word. In reality, that is all I need. If I worry or stress, it is because I am taking on things that are not mine to take on. Help me lay these things at your feet and remain in you. Amen.

Respond

- When you feel as if you are entering a battle, what is your first instinct?

- How can you strengthen your faith to help you stand tall and face your daily battles head-on?

- Can you remember a time of crisis that resulted better than you ever imagined? How can you use this as a reminder that God's ways are better than our ways?

Week 4: Day 2

BETTER LATTE THAN NEVER

By Jessica Casarez

Scripture Reading

[1] For everything there is a season, and a time for every matter under heaven

Ecclesiastes 3:1

Thoughts for the Day

I did not become a Christian until the ripe age of twenty-four. I grew up in a Catholic home and for many years my perception of God was that he only existed inside the walls of the church building and we only visited him on Sundays. I had never read the Bible until my husband—who was my boyfriend at the time—bought me one. I will never forget the day that I stood up to receive Christ into my heart. I was so scared but I knew I was doing the right thing.

Since that day, my transformation evolved quickly. I hungered for God immensely and wanted everyone to know of this great love I had recently discovered. I prayed for many people. I took friends to church.

But one thought always bothered me: Why hadn't I done this sooner? Why did it take me so long to start living a life with Christ?

This would bother me tremendously and it started making me feel inferior to other Christians who had grown up knowing Christ. Until one day I finally had this realization: I was not saved too late, and neither was I saved too early. It happened at the exact right time it was supposed to happen. When I accepted Christ, God turned everything that had happened *to* me when I was living a life of darkness into things that happened *for* me. These things suddenly gave me a stronger purpose and desire to help others. My passion to share the Gospel stemmed from the fact that I knew how empty your life could be without it!

Friends, I know some of you are living a life of resentment because of an unanswered prayer or perhaps because of something that you think happened too late. Can I encourage you with something? God has appointed the perfect time for everything in your life. Even when things do unfold according to your timeline, you can still enjoy the beauty of it. For me, I had to learn to stop living under the shadow of the twenty-three years that I lived without God as the center of my life. Instead, I made the decision to use the future years of my life to live more intently for God. I am nowhere near perfect but I do know that God has allowed me to live a life richer than I ever imagined these past ten years. But it started with me accepting the fact that God's timing is always perfect.

Invitation to Prayer

Dear Lord: I thank you that your timing is always perfect. Help me remember to stop focusing on my clock but to trust that, in the midst of any chaos that I face, you have already worked out a solution. Help me to stop reminiscing on any past mistakes so I can treasure the joy and peace you have given me today! Your answered prayers are never late but are always on time. I love you so much Lord and I am grateful for your timing. Amen.

Respond

- What is something in your life that you have been spending too much time and energy complaining of its timing?

- How can you work on making sure you trust God's clock over your own?

- Can you think of a time where you are grateful God did not do things in the timing that you desired?

Week 4: Day 3

DEPRESSO

By Jessica Casarez

Scripture Reading

[7] Answer me quickly, O Lord! My spirit fails! Hide not your face from me, lest I be like those who go down to the pit. [8] Let me hear in the morning of your steadfast love, for in you I trust. Make me know the way I should go, for to you I lift up my soul.

Psalm 143:7-8

Thoughts for the Day

I consider myself to be a very joyful person. In fact, I think if you were to survey my friends and family, the majority of them would agree with that statement.

However, from time to time, I find myself feeling a bit down and depressed. Sometimes it is not even due to the circumstances around me. I just feel this dark gloomy cloud hovering over me that is trying to dampen my heart with grief. Sometimes I am filled with the urge to cry and I have no reason to justify what I feel.

Then I stop to think for a minute: "When is the last time I spent some one-on-one time with my Father?" More often than not, that will end up being my diagnosis. I cannot be a light in the world if I do not take the time to fill my own spiritual cup. Not only will I not be a light, but depression will try to completely dim me out.

I realize at times we will face severe situations that may cause our faith to be shaken. But friends, I hope you realize that in those moments, we must cling to God like never before. Depression is not part of God's plan. We must walk forward knowing that nothing we endure has taken God by surprise. He promises to walk by our side and help us overcome anything we might face.

I experienced a miscarriage less than a year ago. Prior to that, I felt as if my life had never been better. Everything seemed to be going in our favor. Our marriage was strong. Our family was thriving. Then we found out we were pregnant with our third child. Perfect! This was the peak of my happiness! But a week later I found out I miscarried and my world came crumbling down. I remember crying tears of anguish in a way I had never experienced before.

I was mourning the loss of a child I never met. I did not know how to survive this tragedy. However, I am so thankful that in the midst of this pain, God's voice was so loud and clear. He allowed me to cry and mourn but one instruction I remember so clearly is this: Do not REMAIN in your PAIN!

God mourns with us. He is a loving and gentle Father. But he will walk with us to *overcome* our grief from loss and tragedies. He doesn't expect us to do it on our own strength. He wants us to rely on him instead of turning our back on him. Ultimately, he will be able to use our pain for his purpose.

Invitation to Prayer

Dear Lord: Thank you for every single season of my life. I know some things will be difficult to comprehend and I may never fully understand the *why* to every single painful question. Help me to just focus on the *who*. I never have to overcome these painful situations in my life alone, because you are with me. Help me to never remain in the pain! I want to be free so others can see what you have done in me! Thank you for your embrace in both the good and bad times. Amen.

Respond

- Have you ever felt depressed? How do you usually combat it?

- What does God's Word say about overcoming depression?

- Sometimes people we love are depressed. Although we want to snap them out of it, this is something they must work through themselves. How can we help a person we love see God's face amid depression?

Week 4: Day 4

COMPARISON COFFEE

By Jessica Casarez

Scripture Reading

[13] For you formed my inward parts; you knitted me together in my mother's womb. [14] I praise you, for I am fearfully and wonderfully made. Wonderful are your works; my soul knows it very well. [15] My frame was not hidden from you, when I was being made in secret, intricately woven in the depths of the earth. [16] Your eyes saw my unformed substance; in your book were written, every one of them, the days that were formed for me, when as yet there was none of them.

Psalm 139:13-16

Thoughts for the Day

The word "comparison" alone still makes me cringe a bit. Can anyone else relate? I struggled with comparison for MANY years. I was constantly comparing myself with other women and often I ended up feeling inferior.

Theodore Roosevelt once said some very true and profound words: "Comparison is the thief of joy." Combine that with John 10:10 that says, "The thief comes only to steal, kill and destroy." Those two statements let you know that comparison is something that the enemy uses against us to immobilize us and to belittle us.

We can try and avoid it as much as possible, but unless we deal with our insecurities, they will come back and inflict some pain on us one way or another.

Why do we do it? Why do we compare ourselves to others? If someone has a smaller waistline than us, can we not be happy for them without sulking about the overstay of the unwanted pounds on our own body? Why do we want colored eyes instead of appreciating the dark eyes we were born with? Why are we threatened if another person starts a successful blog or sings well?

The bottom line is this: God created every single one of us uniquely. It is not a disadvantage to look the way we look. The gifts we possess are not gifts we gained by chance. God purposely gave these to us and created us exactly as he intended.

One of my biggest battles with comparison has dealt with physical traits. I always felt like the ugly duckling in school compared to the other girls. I always felt as if I was not good enough. Someone was always prettier, always skinnier, or always smarter. I was drowning in a pool of misery. But then one day I realized I was the one adding all the water, and I was had the power to turn it off! I simply had to stop constantly comparing myself with others.

The more time I spent resenting what I did not have, the more time I wasted neglecting what I did possess. I was letting the enemy win! I was letting him steal my job and rob me of my purpose, all because I had allowed the poison of comparison to consume me. But no more! I am now fully aware that God created me perfectly. No, I am not perfect. His design is perfect. I will simply rejoice in how he made me because I know I could never imagine or design anything better than God.

Invitation to Prayer

Dear Lord: Thank you for designing me so perfectly. I have learned to embrace all my imperfections because I know that you use everything in my life for good. While I may be tempted to compare myself to others from time to time, I thank you for your reassurance that there is nobody else that is just like me. You designed me just as I am for a purpose. My flaws have a reason. And my delight comes from only you. Amen.

Respond

- What do you struggle the most with when it comes to comparison?

- We keep thieves out of our homes by locking our doors and installing an alarm. How can we lock our minds to not allow the enemy to steal our joy through comparison?

- What are you grateful for about how God has designed and created you?

Week 4: Day 5

PRESSING THROUGH PRIDE

By Leah Whitton

Scripture Reading

[3] Do nothing from selfish ambition or conceit, but in humility count others more significant than yourselves.

Philippians 2:3

Thoughts for the Day

Everyone can see it in us, except us: pride. Pride shows up in many ways and our society often glorifies it. Everywhere you go, you hear people admonishing that you should have pride in your work, pride in your school, pride in your kids, pride in sports, and the list goes on. Society portrays pride as a good characteristic. The problem with pride is that it is self-deceiving. Pride is sneaky and many times we don't recognize that it can become a major problem as it leads to selfishness and thinking of ourselves more highly than we should.

I wish I could say I learned how to deal with pride at an early age, but it wasn't until my late thirties that I truly began to see that I had an issue with this. Pride haunted me and consumed me at my work place, at my church, and at my home. I competed against those around me, constantly aiming to be recognized as the best at everything I did.

One day, my husband very gently mentioned that I may have a root of pride down deep in my heart. I was gentle in my response back to my husband… NOT. I was defensive and upset that he would say such a thing. But if I am honest, I knew he was telling the truth. I was too prideful to admit he was right. It was a hard season to walk through as I realized I was a prideful person and I started letting God help me squeeze out the pride in my life. What did I do? I cried for a very long time, and then I started to pray. I prayed for months asking God to humble me and rip out pride from every part of my life. I am thankful to my God of grace that walked with me through it all. I can now often recognize pride when it comes up and I immediately start battling against it. I pray and do my best to think of "What would Jesus do?" and try my best to follow.

The Bible has a lot to say about pride and how to overcome it. James 4:6 says, "God opposes the proud but gives grace to the humble." James 4:10 reminds us to "humble yourselves before the Lord, and he will exalt you." Philippians 2:3 states, "Do nothing from selfish ambition or conceit, but in humility count others more significant than yourselves." Scripture after scripture tells us to become humble. We must make a choice to make decisions with humility, love others above ourselves, work with humility, and serve in humility.

When you spend time with Jesus and get to know Him, you begin to take on his characteristics. The best representation of humility is Jesus himself. He literally came down from heaven to serve us and to die for our sins so that we could live forever with him. He denied himself for others. Powerful!

Want to grow in humility? Want to stop living a prideful life? Get on your knees at the coffee table today, humble yourself, and ask God to reveal areas in your life that are prideful. As he reveals, repent and ask forgiveness. Then, start walking in humility and obedience.

Invitation to Prayer

Dear Lord: Thank you for loving me and giving me grace when I fall and stumble. I admit I have been dealing with the issue of pride in my life. Deliver me from pride's grip. Help me to give myself to you and to listen to your Word. I want to walk in a humble manner at home, at my job, at church, or wherever I go. Help me to walk this out and recognize and resist every temptation to be prideful. Amen.

Respond

- What are characteristics of a prideful person?

- What are the characteristics of a humble person?

- Is God revealing areas in your life where you are prideful? What are they? What do you need to do to defeat it?

Week 5

JESUS AND COFFEE TIME

Week 5: Day 1

CONFLICTED COFFEE

By Leah Whitton

Scripture Reading

[1] A soft answer turns away wrath, but a harsh word stirs up anger.

Proverbs 15:1

[26] Be angry and do not sin; do not let the sun go down on your anger,

Ephesians 4:26

[15] "If your brother sins against you, go and tell him his fault, between you and him alone. If he listens to you, you have gained your brother.

Matthew 18:15

Thoughts for the Day

You know the feeling. You can feel it in the pit of your stomach. It makes you feel sick thinking about it. It is the feeling of conflict.

Conflict can be very emotional and hurtful. It can impact you physically, mentally, emotionally, and spiritually. The question is not whether conflict will come, but *when* will it come and how will we handle it? Conflict happens wherever there are people involved, whether it be at home, work, school, or church.

Often, we try to avoid conflict because we worry about hurting other's feelings, but God gave us clear direction on how to deal with conflict biblically.

The Bible tells us "as it depends on you, live peaceably with all" (Romans 12:18). Sometimes that is not easy. In fact, it can be incredibly difficult! I remember as a young pastor's wife being dealt my first experience with church conflict. I had overheard someone talking about my husband in a derogatory way and everything in me at that moment raged. I felt my whole body burn with righteous anger. Everything I had learned about grace up to this point simply left my mind. I busted into the room and gave them a mouthful of why they shouldn't be gossiping and then slammed the door behind me. This was extremely out of character for me, but nonetheless, the conflict had started and I had made it worse. I was now a part of the problem. I graciously went back a few minutes later and humbled myself and asked for forgiveness. At that moment, we were able to talk and discuss so we could resolve the situation biblically. I could have easily just left, kept it unresolved, talked to others about the situation; but instead, I chose to humble myself.

We can resolve conflicts by submitting to God unconditionally and putting him first. We need to put ourselves under God's covering and sovereignty every day. Learn to fully trust him, read his Word, and obey.

One of the most important things we can do is sincerely pray for the person that has offended us. After praying, talk directly to the person and believe the best in them. "If your brother sins against you, go and tell him his fault, between you and him alone. If he listens to you, you have gained your brother" (Matthew 18:15). Explain your side, but try not to cast blame. Remember you can't avoid conflict, but you can approach it biblically. Submit and humble yourself to God, pray for all involved in the conflict, and lastly let God guide you as you talk to the people involved instead of just avoiding them.

Is there someone in your life that you are having conflict with? Will you pray for them and for the situation believing God will resolve it?

Invitation to Prayer

Dear Lord: Help me put you first in every area of my life so when conflict comes I can handle it according to your Word. I humble myself today and ask forgiveness if I have caused the conflict. Help me make it right. Lord, help me to never be one to avoid conflict or unnecessarily start conflict. I know you say to try to live at peace with everyone. Help me walk that out today and every day. I submit myself to you and thank you for giving me peace while I am walking through conflict. Amen.

Respond

- When conflict comes up, what is your first reaction? Why?

- What does God tell us to do when faced with conflict?

- How did Jesus face conflict? Give examples.

Week 5: Day 2

SHADE-GROWN COFFEE

By Leah Whitton

Scripture Reading

⁵ The Lord is your keeper; the Lord is your shade on your right hand. ⁶ The sun shall not strike you by day, nor the moon by night. ⁷ The Lord will keep you from all evil; he will keep your life. ⁸ The Lord will keep your going out and your coming in from this time forth and forevermore.

Psalm 121:5-8

Thoughts for the Day

I had never heard of shade-grown coffee until recently. Apparently, some coffee producers grow their coffee under shade to add certain benefits. Growing it this way requires little or no chemical fertilizers or pesticides making it healthier for you.

Perhaps we can learn something from shade-grown coffee. God says multiple times in the Bible that he is our shade and covering. What if we became shade-grown Christians? What if we decided to intentionally get under God's authority and protective covering every day? Perhaps it would change us and protect us and make us spiritually healthier.

There is such deep truth in Psalm 121:5-8. This scripture was written as a "song of ascent" or a traveling song for the Jewish people on a journey. As they faced difficulties on their journey, they would sing these verses to remind them of who was watching over them.

At a recent track event for my oldest son, we were sitting in the bleachers when suddenly a storm came upon us. Thankfully, my husband saw the ominous clouds in the distance and quickly grabbed the umbrella from the car. He retrieved it just in time before the rain started to pour down on us. We both bent down to gather as close to under the umbrella to protect us from getting soaked. The storm quickly passed and we were kept dry.

I like to think of God as our spiritual umbrella or shade. For an umbrella to work, you must be close underneath it or you will be exposed to the elements around you. God's Word is very clear that he will protect you, but you must get close under God.

The umbrella we used at the track meet was also big enough to cover us. Could you imagine standing in the rain with a tiny umbrella in your hand? You would get pounded! This goes to show us that spiritually, we must get under an umbrella that is much bigger than us or it will be of no use. We can't do this life journey with all its distractions and pain without our big God. Just as an umbrella protects us from the rain that falls upon us, God wants to be our safe place, our strong tower, and our shade from the things of the world that attack us. Proverbs 18:10 says, "The name of the Lord is a strong tower; the righteous man runs into it and is safe."

Will you let him be your strong tower—your shade? Psalm 91:1 tells us, "He who dwells in the shelter of the Most High will abide in the shadow of the Almighty." Let's be shade-grown Christians that abide under God's protection, trusting God every day to keep us no matter what we face on this journey of life.

Invitation to Prayer

Dear Lord: Let me be a Christian that will abide under the shadow of your wings. I understand that I need to be close to you and place you above all things. Thank you for watching over me every day. Help me be a shade-grown Christian, always submitting to you and remaining underneath your shade of protection for my life. Amen.

Respond

- Are you abiding underneath God's shade?

- After reading Psalms 91, what does the Bible tell us about abiding under the shadow of his wings?

- Have you placed God above everything else? If not, what have you placed there instead?

Week 5: Day 3

FLAVORED COFFEE

By Leah Whitton

Scripture Reading

[4] For as in one body we have many members, and the members do not all have the same function, [5] so we, though many, are one body in Christ, and individually members one of another.

Romans 12:4-5

Thoughts for the Day

My first year of teaching at an elementary school was definitely a learning experience. I had a lot of questions, anxieties, and unknowns. I thought I was the only one feeling this and kept it to myself. Boy, was I wrong. Many of the new teachers at our school that year felt the same way. I was paired up with a mentor teacher that gracefully took my hand and helped me survive my first year of teaching. My mentor teacher had gifts, experience, and knowledge that I had not yet gained. She made my first year much easier. When we worked together, I was stronger.

We should desire to be around people that have a different flavor than us. What I mean by that is: Surround yourself with people that have different gifts, experiences, and knowledge.

We need to develop a team mentality. All of us should recognize our limitations and seek those who have gifts and talents different from us. We should also recognize that God has given each of us unique gifts to use for him so that we can serve others. When you add your gifts with many others, much can be accomplished.

When I think of teamwork, I visualize the Olympic sport of rowing. The synchronization of each eight-member team is simply amazing to watch. At the head of the rowboat is someone who is called the coxswain. It is the coxswain's job to lead, steer, and motivate the rest of the rowers in the boat. The rowers must put their complete trust in the coxswain. The rowers all have a unique job and all are important. They all need and rely on each other to get them to the finish line.

Imagine, God as the coxswain in the front of the rowboat. Can we get in the boat, let God lead, and be unified using our different gifts for a common goal? We all need each other to get to the finish line. Psalm 133:1 says, "Behold, how good and pleasant it is when [God's people] dwell in unity!" 1 Peter 3:8 declares, "Finally, all of you, have unity of mind, sympathy, brotherly love, a tender heart, and a humble mind." God is talking to the church; God is telling us to be unified.

When I think of a unifying force, I think of the battle of Jericho found in Joshua 6:1-2. The Israelites joined together and marched around the city of Jericho for seven days, and on the seventh day marched seven times again. Then, with a loud unified shout—everyone's voice unique yet all unified in their mission—the walls of Jericho crumbled down. Wow! What if the church was completely united that all we had to do was shout at the walls of division, racism, jealousy, and pride and see the walls crumble before us. We are a mighty force when we unite under Christ and use our gifts to serve others.

Put God first. Let him lead. Then listen, obey, and follow as a unified team. God designed us to need him *and* each other. We were not intended to do this all on our own. So, during your coffee break this morning, think of ways how you can use your gifts to help others and how you can be a part of a unified team. We must all do our part.

Invitation to Prayer

Dear Lord: I understand the importance of being a part of a team. Thank you for placing people in my life that have unique gifts that help me on my walk with you. Help me know what my gifts are so that I may use them to bless others. If there are situations in my life where I am causing division, forgive me and help me to see my fellow Christians as a close-knit team, unified under you. Help us to listen to you as you lead your unified people. Amen.

Respond

- What does teamwork mean according to the Bible? Can you think of a team you could model after?

- What are the gifts God gave you to use and to serve others with?

- When you think of unity, what is the first thing that comes to mind? How can you walk this type of unity out daily in your life?

Week 5:
Day 4

BARISTA BLUES

By Jessica Casarez

Scripture Reading

[9] As the Father has loved me, so have I loved you. Abide in my love. [10] If you keep my commandments, you will abide in my love, just as I have kept my Father's commandments and abide in his love. [11] These things I have spoken to you, that my joy may be in you, and that your joy may be full.

John 15:9-11

Thoughts for the Day

I love trying different coffee places. Not only that, I love becoming friends with the baristas that work at the coffee houses I frequent. Over the years, I have had the privilege of meeting so many and most of them end up knowing what I am going to order as soon as I step inside the building or go through the drive thru.

Baristas have a special place in my heart. They control the temperature and taste of my drink. It can be too hot or too cold if they are not focused. It can be too sweet or too bitter if they are too rushed.

I sometimes like to consider myself like a barista. No, I have no idea how to whip up a double chocolate chip Frappuccino with a triple shot that is light on the foam. However, as the woman of my house, I often control the "tone" of our house. Have you heard the phrase "Happy Wife, Happy Life?" Well, when I am happy, my joy is contagious and everyone in our house will often also be in a good mood. But on the days when I have allowed the enemy to get the best of me, it sets a completely different tone in the house. The kids are grouchy and crying and my husband is finding any excuse to leave the house and avoid me. Or even worse, sometimes he mimics my angry behavior which just creates a crazy and angry cycle.

Sometimes my joy evades me because of everything that must be done. I do all the cleaning, cooking, laundry, etc. There are days where I just want someone else to do it all! I begin to complain and throw a tantrum that can put my three-year-old to shame!

But I have realized that when I do that, I am minimizing my blessings. You see, as a little girl, I *dreamed* of being married and being a stay-at-home mommy. It was what my mom did and I always wanted to grow up to be just like her. And if I take a step back, I am living a very blessed life! But when I view it from a perspective of disdain and focus on each day's little problems, it minimizes all the blessings God has given me.

I once heard someone say, "Right now, someone out there is praying for the same thing that you are cursing in your life."

I have some friends who would *love* to be able to have children to clean up after! I have some friends who can't wait to get married and have dinner ready when their husbands come home! And yet, there I am, living the life they are praying for but wasting God's blessings because I am spending all my energy complaining about my blessings.

My favorite baristas are the ones who are cheerful as they make my hot drink or cool beverage. No matter how long the lines are at the coffee house, they always seem to keep it together with a joyful spirit. That is how I want to run my household and love my family—with joy and gratitude in my heart no matter what.

Invitation to Prayer

Dear Lord: Thank you for reminding me that my blessings are not burdens. I do not want my joy to be conditional. Help me to appreciate everything that you have given me, even when I am tired or frustrated. Remind me that even on my very worst days there is someone who is praying and waiting for the blessings you have already given to me in my life. May my joy be unwavering so I can resist the urge to complain and invite unwanted emotions in our household and in my heart. Amen.

Respond

- What is something that often causes you to lose your joy at home?

- When you are in a bad mood, how do other people around you respond, whether at home or at work?

- What can you do to better hold onto your joy regardless of your circumstances?

Week 5:
Day 5

ARTIFICIAL SWEETNESS

By Jessica Casarez

Scripture Reading

[25] To whom then will you compare me, that I should be like him? says the Holy One. [26] Lift up your eyes on high and see: who created these? He who brings out their host by number, calling them all by name; by the greatness of his might and because he is strong in power, not one is missing.

Isaiah 40:25-26

Thoughts for the Day

I love having a cup of coffee every single morning. It is a part of my daily routine no matter what. But occasionally I am disappointed to find out I have run out of creamer! I personally love my coffee with A LOT of creamer. I mean A LOT. A few times I have had to try and substitute the creamer with other things in my fridge or pantry. The result is always the same: Nothing compares to my creamer. I never enjoy my coffee as much when I run out of creamer. It just isn't the same.

I had a similar revelation a couple of years ago, except about something so much bigger. You see, my husband and I gave our lives to Christ many years ago. However, when we had children, for some reason church took a backseat. We stopped going to church and convinced ourselves that we were seasoned enough to stay strong in our faith.

Talk about complete foolishness! This was a time where we needed to be seeking the Lord more than ever. We were young parents, living with these little people who kept trying to follow us and learn from us. We were not ready for this at all. In fact, with both of my children, I fell into a stage of postpartum depression shortly after their birth. It was a miserable season of feeling so alienated and hopeless. But remember: We were not attending church then, so we had become easy targets.

A friend suggested painting our walls yellow to bring some cheer back into our lives. We not only took her suggestion but we ran with it! We painted our living room, our bathrooms, and our kitchen yellow! In hindsight, I am a little surprised we actually did this and more surprised my husband went along with it. But I am sure he was tired of living with a depressed wife who usually had a spirit of joy.

This is the part where I am supposed to tell you that our plan unfolded perfectly and the depression instantly left me. That was not the case at all. In fact, I think my depression got worse!

Now that I look back at all of this, I realize that I was trying to replace the Son with the sun. I thought bringing yellow walls in the house would fill the darkness I was feeling with bright light. The only problem with that is that nothing can fill our hearts and spirits like Christ. Our human efforts can only do so much, but there are no limits to what God can do.

So, we began to pray fervently for God to lead us to the right church, and He delivered like only he can. We found our church home where we were welcomed with amazing pastors whom we call our friends. Slowly but surely, that heavy depression left me and was replaced with a newfound zest for life. My husband and I will forever be grateful that we never settled for artificial happiness but instead continued our pursuit for more—for the real deal! We realized that there truly is nothing that can satisfy our hunger for God but God Himself!

Invitation to Prayer

Dear Lord: Thank you for being a Father who is the real deal. There is nobody and nothing else that compares to you! Even when we stray and try to substitute other things for your love, you patiently await our return with open arms. I love you so much God. I have seen with my own eyes how dark and miserable life is without your constant presence. Never allow me to give in to pride that makes me think I don't need you. As long as I have breath in my lungs, may my desire be for you above all else. Amen.

Respond

- Have you ever tried to substitute Christ with someone or something else in your life?

- How did that make you feel?

- What can we do to ensure we don't settle for artificial happiness instead of a real relationship with Jesus?

Week 6

MY CUP OVERFLOWS

Week 6: Day 1

A CUPFUL OF FORGIVENESS

By Leah Whitton

Scripture Reading

[21] Then Peter came up and said to him, "Lord, how often will my brother sin against me, and I forgive him? As many as seven times?" [22] Jesus said to him, "I do not say to you seven times, but seventy-seven times.

[23] "Therefore the kingdom of heaven may be compared to a king who wished to settle accounts with his servants. [24] When he began to settle, one was brought to him who owed him ten thousand talents. [25] And since he could not pay, his master ordered him to be sold, with his wife and children and all that he had, and payment to be made. [26] So the servant fell on his knees, imploring him, 'Have patience with me, and I will pay you everything.' [27] And out of pity for him, the master of that servant released him and forgave him the debt. [28] But when that same servant went out, he found one of his fellow servants who owed him a hundred denarii, and seizing him, he began to choke him, saying, 'Pay what you owe.' [29] So his fellow servant fell down and pleaded with him, 'Have patience with me, and I will pay you.' [30] He refused and went and

put him in prison until he should pay the debt. [31] When his fellow servants saw what had taken place, they were greatly distressed, and they went and reported to their master all that had taken place. [32] Then his master summoned him and said to him, 'You wicked servant! I forgave you all that debt because you pleaded with me. [33] And should not you have had mercy on your fellow servant, as I had mercy on you?' [34] And in anger his master delivered him to the jailers, until he should pay all his debt. [35] So also my heavenly Father will do to every one of you, if you do not forgive your brother from your heart."

Matthew 18:21-35

Thoughts for the Day

Stick with me today on this sticky issue as we dive deep about forgiving others. I have talked to people about this issue more than any other issue in life. It constantly comes up in counseling sessions, prayer times, and conversations. Unforgiveness is one issue that truly keeps people locked in the bondage of bitterness and hurt without even realizing it.

Forgiving someone is not an easy thing to do. It is the main reason most of us don't. We often would rather seek revenge than forgive someone. It's just a part of our human nature. If you hurt me, I will hurt you back. Have you ever thought or said those words before? Perhaps you have experienced pain in a marriage, divorce, a wrong business deal, a hurtful friendship, or even someone saying untrue things about you. This list could go on. I often hear people say things like, "You don't know how bad they hurt me," or "You don't know the terrible things they said," or "They haven't apologized and I won't either." We have a lot of reasons and excuses why we won't forgive. I have experienced many times in my life where I didn't feel like forgiving, but I chose to forgive anyway.

I referenced earlier in this book that my only sister was tragically killed in a drunk driving accident back in 2012. The young man that killed her was unrepentant and even blamed someone else for the accident. To this day, I have not received or heard the words, "I'm sorry." I cannot tell you the pain it has caused me and my family and how heartbroken I still feel. I wake up every day missing my sister—wanting to call her just to hear her voice—only to remember that I can't. The tears are real and the hurt still rests on my heart.

Seeing my parents journey through the difficult and horrifying season of losing their daughter was heartbreaking but also gave me a powerful example to follow. They walked and are still walking through the pain, leaning on God's amazing love and gentle compassion. They graciously have shown forgiveness and love through it all, and their faith in God has proven unshakable.

Although I could have easily become very bitter and unforgiving towards the man that killed my sister, I chose to forgive him. Forgiving isn't easy and it took some time, but God never said it would be easy. He just said to forgive just like he has forgiven us. If Christ can forgive someone like me, who am I to withhold forgiveness from someone else.

In the story found in Matthew 18:21-35, we learn a great lesson about forgiveness. A king removed all debt from one of his servants, but that same servant refused to forgive those that owed him a *much* smaller amount of money. Ultimately, he faced terrible consequences from his unwillingness to forgive others.

One thing I have learned over the years is that forgiving does not mean that you make excuses for the other person or gloss over their wrongdoing. When you minimize the wrong, you cheapen the forgiveness. The young man who killed my sister is serving time for what he did and my prayer is he finds God in prison. There are always consequences to making the wrong choice. My job is to forgive and give my hurt to God. Forgiveness is simply releasing your desire to seek revenge, but in releasing that, ultimately it's you that are freed. If I hold a grudge or don't forgive, I am only hurting myself.

An unknown author once said, "Forgiveness is like setting a prisoner free and finding out that prisoner was you." Or maybe you have heard this one quote by another unknown author, "Unforgiveness is like drinking poison and hoping the other person will die." Take a big gulp of forgiveness today and choose to forgive and set yourself free. Forgive and release the hurt to God.

Invitation to Prayer

Dear Lord: I come to you today asking that you forgive me for harboring unforgiveness in my heart. It has slowly eaten up my joy and I am filled with bitterness. Help my heart to heal and help me to hand over all my emotions into your hands. I realize I am only hurting myself when I choose not to forgive. Help me to forgive like you have forgiven me. I know that I can be set free when I choose to forgive. Amen.

Respond

- Why is forgiveness important? Read Matthew 6:14.

- Do you have someone you need to forgive?

- How are you made free when you forgive?

Week 6: Day 2

SPRINKLE IN A LITTLE SWEETNESS

By Jessica Casarez

Scripture Reading

[3] As an apple tree among the trees of the forest, so is my beloved among the young men. With great delight I sat in his shadow, and his fruit was sweet to my taste. [4] He brought me to the banqueting house, and his banner over me was love. [5] Sustain me with raisins; refresh me with apples, for I am sick with love.

Song of Solomon 2:3-5

Thoughts for the Day

While many people assume that Song of Solomon can only be applied in a romantic way, I often find myself using this verse to thank God for dear friends in my life.

I have been very blessed to have an army of amazing friends in my life whom I love and cherish. My friendship with each one of them is special and unique, including the special friendship I have with my husband.

Since coffee happens to be my love language, I love to invite my dear friends out on coffee dates. Sometimes we go in groups and sometimes it is one-on-one. Regardless, I truly delight in my time with my friends. The coffee is simply an added bonus. But I find that these moments are crucial to maintaining strong and healthy friendships.

It is easy to become bombarded and neglect our friends. I don't want to reach out to them only when I need their help. I want to shower them with love and appreciation.

This has also become especially true for my husband. He is my very best friend. But there are seasons where I neglect to cherish him and relish his company. Do you know what happens when I do this? Instead of being blessed by his presence, I start becoming annoyed by him. Every single thing he says or does begins to drive me crazy. But that is because we have failed to set apart that time for us.

Every relationship, friendship, or marriage or even our relationship with God, needs that regular special time of sweetness. All of us run low from time to time. But when we make the effort to refill that cup of sweetness with our sweet friends and loved ones, we are doing exactly what God called us to do: love others.

Invitation to Prayer

Dear Lord: Thank you for enriching my life with beautiful and sweet people. Help me to never take any of them for granted and to set apart those special moments where I can show them how loved and appreciated they are. I realize every single one of them is a gift from you, and you only give your children your very best! Whether it is a coffee date, a play date, or a letter in the mail, help me sprinkle in some sweetness in their lives to reflect your love and kindness. Amen.

Respond

- Do you struggle with making time for the people you love?

- What can you do to prioritize these moments with them?

- What is one of the sweetest memories you have of a person you love? How did this impact you?

Week 6:
Day 3

MY CUP OVERFLOWS WITH THANKFULNESS

By Leah Whitton

Scripture Reading

[18] give thanks in all circumstances; for this is the will of God in Christ Jesus for you.

1 Thessalonians 5:18

Thoughts for the Day

If I were to ask you if you would like to be more thankful, I imagine all of us would say yes. Thankfulness truly affects every part of our lives. It is easy to be thankful when things are going good, but what about when things go wrong?

1 Thessalonians 5:18 says, "Give thanks in all circumstances; for this is the will of God in Christ Jesus for you." Look at these three words again: "IN ALL CIRCUMSTANCES." God is telling us to be thankful in the good times *and* in the bad. Be thankful when you have a good workday or a bad one. Be thankful when money is plentiful or when it is tight. Be thankful *always*!

What are some things we can be thankful for? God's love in Christ Jesus, his grace (undeserved gifts), answered prayers, protection, health, family, and the list can go on and on.

Being thankful in every situation brings honor to God. Psalm 50:23 says, "The one who offers thanksgiving as his sacrifice glorifies me." Thankfulness helps us focus our attention on the best thing: God.

My husband lost his mom several years back to cancer, but my remembrance of her is one of thankfulness. I don't think I have ever met anyone so thankful. Throughout his mom's sickness and pain with the disease, she always had a smile on her face. She lit up any room she was in. Throughout her sickness, we visited her in the hospital and nursing home to brighten her day, but she would always find a way to brighten ours! She was always so thankful to see us and would give us huge hugs and love on us. She understood 1 Thessalonians 5:18 all too well. She lived it. In the middle of her pain and disease, she gave thanks.

Can we thank God in the middle of being sick? That's what he tells us to do. Thank him in *all* things.

Her life was a testimony to so many. At her funeral, when asked if anyone would like to share, dozens upon dozens stood up and shared how she had blessed their lives. Even the nurses that took care of her came and said their lives were changed because of my husband's mom. She lived being thankful no matter what life threw at her.

Does your cup overflow with thankfulness? Choose to be filled with so much of God, that when good or bad things come your way, you will overflow with thankfulness.

Invitation to Prayer

Dear Lord: I choose to thank you today whether my day is good or bad. I will praise you in the middle of my mess, and I will praise you when I am blessed. You know what is best for my family and me. Thank you for your love, grace, and mercy. I will be glad in *all* things and *all* situations starting today. Amen.

Respond

- Start a list of things you are thankful for.

- Read Psalm 50:23 and describe what this verse means to you.

- Describe someone in your life that you have seen be thankful in every situation.

Week 6: Day 4

SWEET AROMA

By Jessica Casarez

Scripture Reading

[1] Oh sing to the Lord a new song; sing to the Lord, all the earth! [2] Sing to the Lord, bless his name; tell of his salvation from day to day. [3] Declare his glory among the nations, his marvelous works among all the peoples! [4] For great is the Lord, and greatly to be praised; he is to be feared above all gods. [5] For all the gods of the peoples are worthless idols, but the Lord made the heavens. [6] Splendor and majesty are before him; strength and beauty are in his sanctuary.

Psalm 96:1-6

Thoughts for the Day

Have you ever attended church and noticed people still streaming into the sanctuary during worship at the beginning of service? Some people could honestly be running late. But others are under the impression that worship is just the opening act before the pastor delivers a great sermon. Nothing could be further from the truth!

Worship is so necessary, God demands it! He wants us to worship him and nobody else.

For me, singing worship music to God is my time to raise my hands and raise my voice to praise him for every single thing he has done in my life.

As I focus on him in worship, I can also listen to his clear instructions. As a writer, I make it a point to carry a notebook with me wherever I go. But often, the Holy Spirit will drop something into my spirit during times of worship. It can be a blog topic. It can be a sentence. Sometimes it can be a single word. Nonetheless, I know it comes from him and I make sure I write it down.

It is also my healing time. Worship is when I cry out to him in the middle of life's chaos. It is when I release that hurt and pain. I release that situation that I cannot control. I release that bitterness and unforgiveness that has been causing me so much anguish. I exchange it for his peace and his promise.

But the beauty of worship is that it does not only take place in the sanctuary. It can happen anywhere—in your car, in your house, or in the gym. We simply need to take time to praise our God who deserves nothing less than our very best.

Consider worship in this manner: When you open the door for someone, do your feelings get hurt if they fail to say thank you? Or when you give someone a gift, would it be considered rude or disrespectful if they failed to acknowledge you? Well, this is exactly what we do when we fail to worship God! Isn't he the one that opens the right doors for us? Doesn't he shower us with his best gifts? Didn't he pay the greatest price for us on the cross? That demands action! It demands praise! It demands worship!

Invitation to Prayer

Dear Lord: Thank you that every good and perfect thing in my life comes from you. Help me to worship you on a new level and to never be complacent about praising you. I want to give you the full honor and glory that you deserve and nothing less. Remove any fear, worry, or distractions that hinder me from worshipping you in the manner that you deserve. Receive my praise and all my love Father. My heart shouts praises to you! Amen.

Respond

- How important would you say worship time has been in your life?

- What are some ways you worship God?

- Do you notice a different in your spirit when you make the time to worship God in the manner that he deserves?

Week 6: Day 5

DOUBLE SHOT OF LOVE

By Leah Whitton

Scripture Reading

[30] And you shall love the Lord your God with all your heart and with all your soul and with all your mind and with all your strength.' [31] The second is this: 'You shall love your neighbor as yourself.' There is no other commandment greater than these."

Mark 12:30-31

Thoughts for the Day

God loves us so much! No matter how bad we have messed up, God loves us! He loves every little part of us and cares about all the details about our lives.

When I was a college student on my way to a garage sale one morning with my mom, I prayed I would find something that I had been wanting. Money was tight and garage sales were my friend every Saturday morning. This particular Saturday was different. I prayed for something very specific: I wanted a hunter green name-brand purse.

Now, I know it was a material item—one that I couldn't afford—but it was something I desired at the time. Do you know that God cares about all the little details about your life? After leaving the last garage sale, I was disappointed. I didn't find the purse I had searched for all day. But, I felt God tell me to turn around and go look again. I wasn't sure if it was my wishful thinking or God's still small voice speaking to my heart, but I turned around and went back to the last garage sale. I truly felt the Holy Spirit guide me to this dirty cardboard box near the back of the garage that the owners had just put out. God spoke to my heart and said look in the bottom of the box. I started digging through the box and at the bottom of the box was the exact purse that I had longed for. I couldn't believe it. I started crying and praising God all at the same time. People around me probably thought I was little crazy, but who wouldn't be? God loved me so much that He would lead me to the exact purse I wanted. I paid five dollars for the purse and in shock made my way to my car. As I opened the purse to look inside, there was a little red Bible inside with these words written, "Because I love you." I broke out with tears of joy and love. At that moment, I understood God's incredible love for me—for every part of me—the bad and the good stuff, the practical stuff, the spiritual stuff, and even the small details.

God loves us so much, he sent his Son to die for our forgiveness (John 3:16), and he continues to pour out his love on us daily.

His great love should compel us to love others also. He tells us in Mark 12:31 that we should love others as ourselves. Let that soak in. Are you loving others like you need to? I still have that little red Bible and it still serves as a reminder of how much I am loved and how much I should love others.

Invitation to Prayer

Dear Lord: Thank you for loving me so much that you sent your Son, Jesus, to die for my sins. Thank you for caring about every detail of my life, big or small. You know the desires of my heart and you are a loving Father. Help me to love others like you love. Open my eyes to those around me that need to feel that love. Amen.

Respond

- Can you describe a time in your life that you deeply felt the love of God?

- Read Mark 12:31 and describe how you should love others.

- How can you love like Jesus loves today? Think of practical ways you can show love and write them down.

Made in the USA
Middletown, DE
15 November 2018